Alone In A Crowded Room

Darren Roberts

Copyright © 2020

ISBN: 9798626987461

Cover picture:
By the author, Juno Beach, 6th June 2019

All other pictures: unsplash.com & Lee Davies

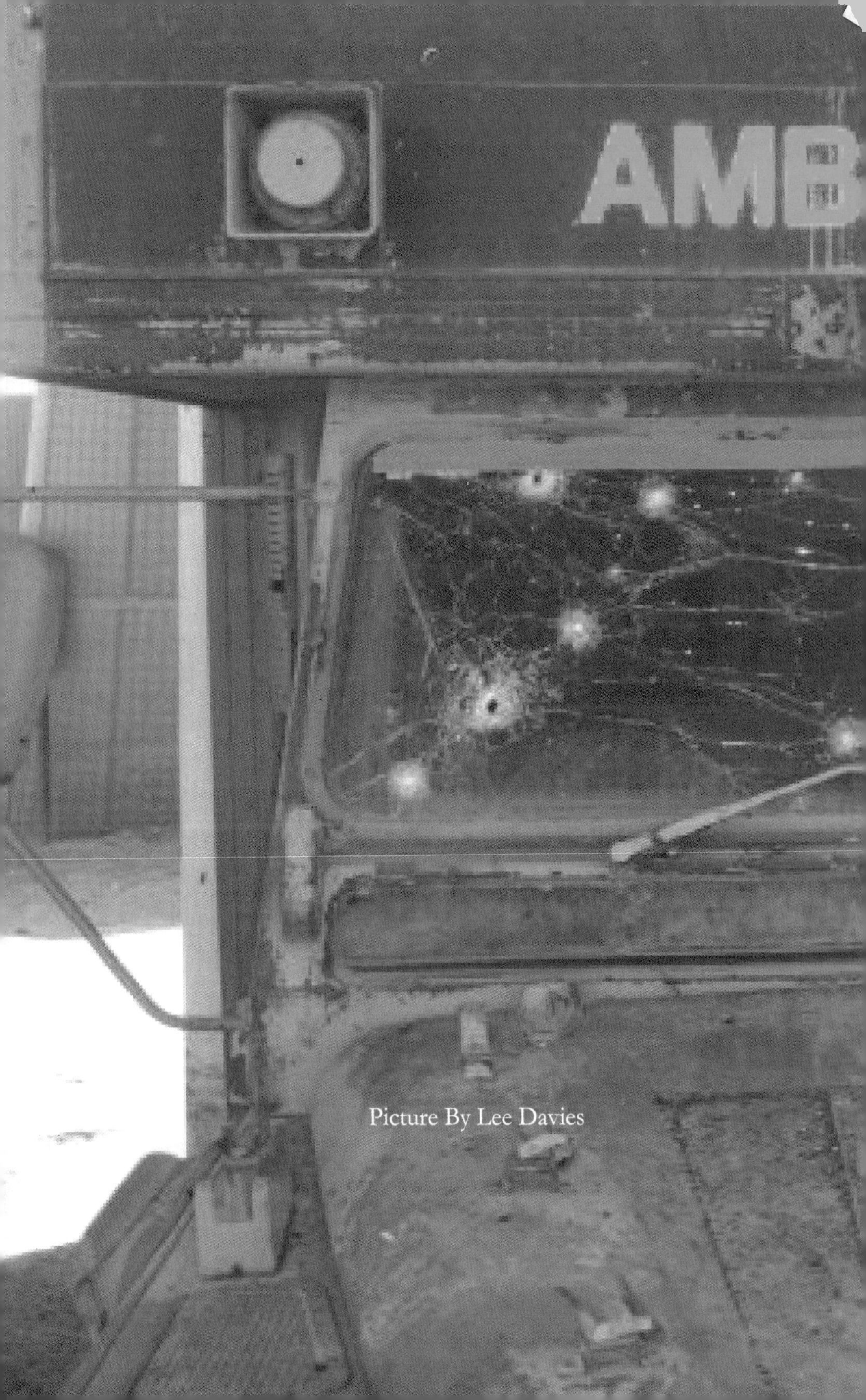

Picture By Lee Davies

Foreword

I was given the privilege of being asked to write this foreword after already being humbled by being asked to contribute. I am one of the authors of the works compiled. I am a British Army combat veteran of the Iraq and Afghanistan conflicts. I have lived, loved, lost, hated and killed in these conflicts. A large part of me was left behind in these lands and what is left is invested in these words.

This book is brutal, raw and retrospective look into service life and conflict directly from the men and women who lived, breathed and bled it. Through poetry and first hand accounts the readers will get an understanding of the duality of man in conflict. The humour that gets the troops through the dark times and the bond between the men and women of service life.

This compilation from the hearts and minds of those that served has been collated by and contributed to by Darren Roberts the author of Sweeping leaves in the wind. Darren is a veteran of the conflicts in Northern Ireland and the Balkans. Darren is deeply invested in helping other veterans and all the proceeds of these works will go to helping veterans in need. Darren is a man I am proud to call a friend and a brother

I thank you for buying this book and contributing to the welfare of veterans in need.

Joe Lyne

Northern Ireland, the main thing from this picture is those 90's fuel prices! Years later watching troops being forced to use the same snatch wagons in Iraq was absolutely infuriating.

They were not fit for purpose in NI, so to see troops being deployed with them in Iraq 10 years after being told all the cut backs were to create a leaner better equipped force were and always have been fucking bullshit. These decisions made by politicians and implemented by the CoC cost lives.

Darren Roberts

Acknowledgments

These are the incredible people that have contributed and help make this book possible;

Neville Johnson, Joe Lyne, Rob 'Smash' Creighton, Lee Davies, Shane Glasspool, Noah Miller, Carolyn Jones, Willam FM Currie, Steve Shepherd & Ben Fleming.

I can't thank you all enough, you gave your help, words and encouragement without hesitation - this is what brother and sisterhood means.

For Those That Can't

I will never forget the feeling watching the bombs drop on Tora Bora in 2001, that feeling was envy, maybe even jealousy. I'd only been out for a couple of years, and the thought of missing an up coming expeditionary war to Afghanistan and the inevitable invasion of Iraq (again) was gutting. Despite joining in 1989 I'd missed the first Gulf War in 1991 by 4 weeks, we were scheduled to go out in April of 1991 but of course it ended so quickly the lads in place stayed on - but not before we ended up having all the injections... We had the date to deploy and who we were to relieve in place. The war ended though, amid the protestations and ultimately prophetic, 'We'll only have to go back and finish it in 10 years'.

The reality for me, and maybe others, is I wanted to go to war, I wanted to fight - I was desperate to go, just 18 years old.

I wanted to kill the 'enemy'.

It's a testament to the training and conditioning I received that I felt that way. Being used to implement illegal and immoral geopolitical policies in a foreign country wasn't something I was even aware of back then. There was an enemy and we were the sovereign power and therefore the good guys coming to save the day. Like the good boy soldier I was, please point me in the direction of the enemy and let me go.

Please, let me go.

I haven't been in a firefight, my tours were limited to the cat & mouse games of Northern Ireland and the impotence of the UN in Bosnia. The abject disappointment I felt when a vehicle did not run a check point,

Beret on for a picture in a field in NI in the mid 90's. CS95 was brand new then, chest rigs were self bought as they were not issued to us.

I ditched the ear piece as it just kept falling out and I couldn't hear shit, but now regret that as it would increase the allyness of the picture by 1000%.

I didn't have my CBA on underneath my smock - it would have done absolutely nothing.

Darren Roberts

when someone did as instructed, when we didn't stumble on someone planting an IED, the weapons caché or able to chase a sniper down. My boy soldier's desire to be in that fight, to be tested and see how I would respond was there, and honestly in some way still is. I still want to kill an enemy that isn't there, to express the training and 9 years of my life from a 16 years old boy. There is no romantic outcome to that, just trauma and pain. I have good friends who have been in a firefight, have killed and yet despite knowing all of that, the ultimate cost to them - I still yearn for it.

I have no way of reasoning or explaining that.

30 years later and my distorted world view of a society lost in instant gratification and Tik-Toks fills me with disdain, yet who am I to judge? Had I stayed in and fought in Afghanistan and Iraq, would I look back at a job well done and a price worth paying? The anger still sits there in me, festering in my mind, the boy soldier wound up like a clockwork toy for a society that doesn't know or care either way. So I fight, but it's not the enemy, it's myself. My family. Friends. Strangers. Anyone really.

I've often wondered if I was simply born in the wrong decade, or even the wrong century. Maybe I should've been at Rourkes Drift or The Charge of The Light Brigade, am I solider out of time trying to make the world fit to some romantic chivalrous nonsense of duty to the flag that doesn't exist anymore. If it ever really existed.

I have no way of reasoning or explaining that.

I cannot stand the cliché image of the broken soldier perennially misunderstood and unable to 'fit into' society. Veterans do not have a monopoly on trauma, there are many civilians and emergency workers

LLP trials, I look about 12
with no scrim on my helmet.

Darren Roberts

that go through extreme trauma leaving them just as vulnerable, helpless and forgotten by the same 'systems' that we bemoan. There is a shared experience which we can find in each other, that can help us to move on in the lives we have and forgive society for its failings. Forgive the corrupt elected political class? That's a **no** from me. That shouldn't hold me or anyone back though, it should spur us on to take action and responsibility for what we CAN do about the place we find ourselves at or in. No one is coming to save us, we have to save ourselves and each other.

Poetry isn't something I ever saw myself writing, not for any other reason than I lacked the creative skill to do it. Putting together the first book 'Sweeping Leaves In The Wind', I was totally inspired by Neville Johnson's words. Here was a soldier trying to make sense of his thoughts, feelings and likely his reality through poetry. There is the antiquity version of the 'warrior poet' and I never fully understood it. How art and war can fit together, stories like The Iliad and Odysseus' journey home to Greece after the Trojan war. How the arts and philosophy formed part of the training of most ancient armies like the Greeks, Spartans and Trojans. There then, was at least some sort of attempt to reconcile what goes on inside a soldiers mind and prepare them for that.

I think I can now see the truth of it, to only really know myself when I let go of my ego and embrace the true philosophical challenges that warfare or being trained for warfare brings. Plato said, "Only the dead see the end of war", something which only now I think I can begin to understand. We're not trained to make sense of our own minds, our thoughts and feelings beyond fighting. Here then, is where poetry seems to bridge that gap, this is why the warrior poet should exist, to help soothe and rationalise the capacity for extreme violence with the ability to care and love.

This is the 2nd in what is hopefully a series of 3 books from The Veteran Collective. If you lay all the books together the covers form a total panoramic shot of Juno Beach taken by me on the 6th June 2019, the 75th Anniversary of the D-Day Landings on those beaches. There will be grammatical errors, missing apostrophes - that's because these are how they were written, mistakes and all.

Here are our stories, thoughts and feelings - simply trying to make sense of the 'why'. Which can help direct us to the 'what' we need to do.

Darren

Explosives dog working the hedgerows in NI. I loved these dogs, loved watching them work and they were always at their happiest when working. The goodest boys....

Darren Roberts

Bosnia mid 90's - A football field was used as a LZ for the Chinooks - often blowing the temporary roofs of the houses, often understandably causing a lot of aggro with the locals. Bosnia mid 90's

Darren Roberts

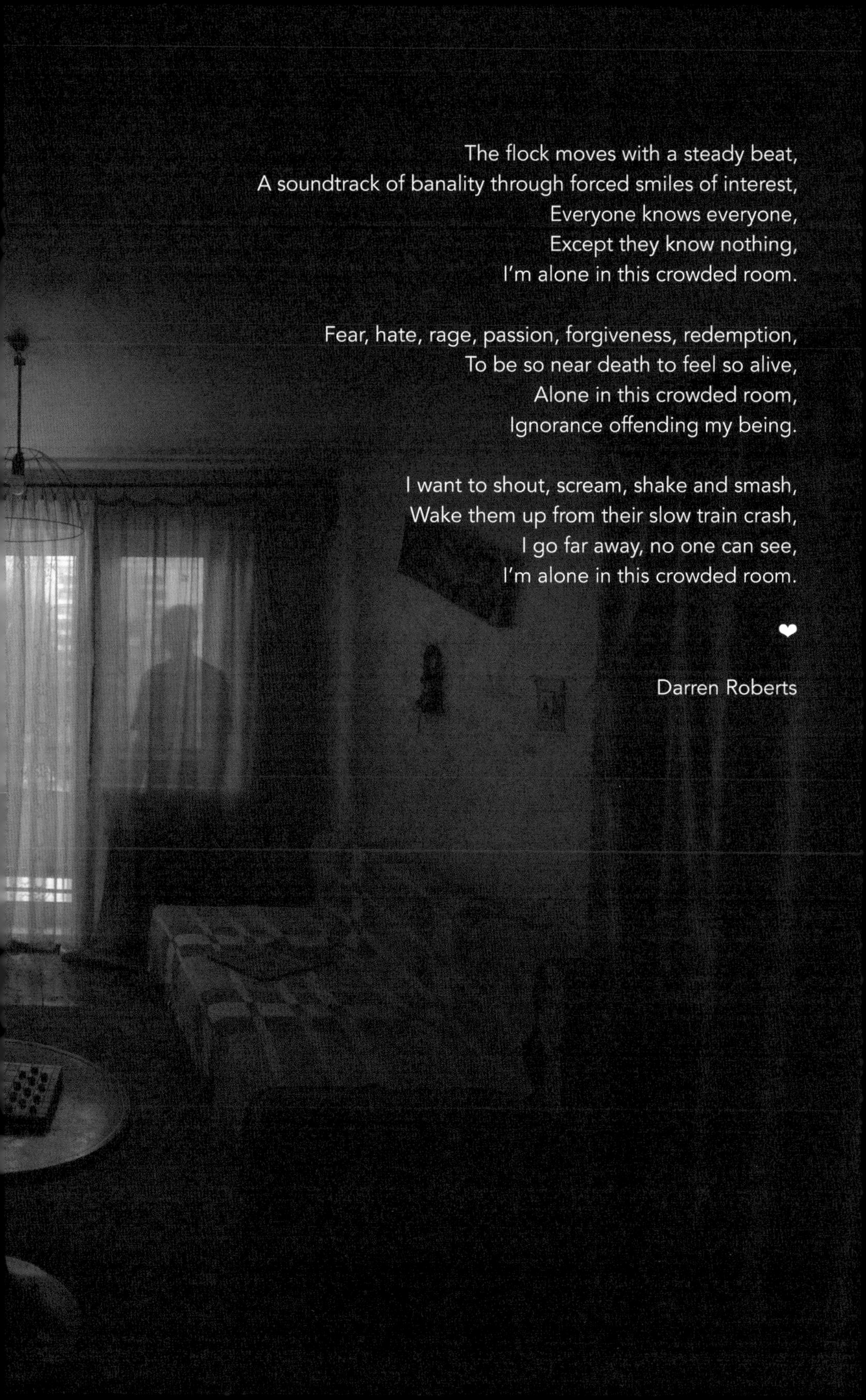

The flock moves with a steady beat,
A soundtrack of banality through forced smiles of interest,
Everyone knows everyone,
Except they know nothing,
I'm alone in this crowded room.

Fear, hate, rage, passion, forgiveness, redemption,
To be so near death to feel so alive,
Alone in this crowded room,
Ignorance offending my being.

I want to shout, scream, shake and smash,
Wake them up from their slow train crash,
I go far away, no one can see,
I'm alone in this crowded room.

❤

Darren Roberts

Fuck Your Press Ups

Darren Roberts

Fuck suicide,
Fuck depression,
Fuck anxiety,
Fuck catastrophising,
Fuck the charities that don't care,
Fuck the system that doesn't want to know,
Fuck the virtue signalling,
Fuck the press ups.

❤

Let us take your only son,
The boy who will be made a man,
Travel the world,
The things he'll see,
We will be his family.

Friends for life,
More than brothers,
We'll always look after him,
Just like all the others,

What a good boy he'll be,
Yes Sir no Sir,
So eager to please,
God, queen and country,
This is the place for him to be.

Let us take your only son,
A good soldier I know he'll be,
That's all he's ever wanted see,
I will make your boy a man,
Look how he wants to come with me,
Oh the things he'll see.

❤

Darren Roberts

The Lies We Believed

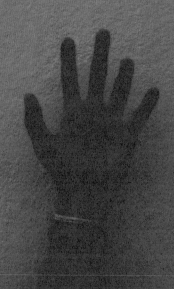

•A QUIET WORD•

Rob Creighton

Brothers,
before you self-diagnose with mental illness,
Take a knee, listen in; I think you should hear this...
Rather than looking for what's wrong with your head,
Take a good look at your life choices instead.
Is your mind sick because of all the booze and the gear,
Instead have a brew and a chat,
help your mind become clear.
Could it be hanging with those lizards and snakes,
The ones who pretend to be friends but are fakes.
Brothers it's time to knock off the drugs, mugs and drink,
Re-org, re-group and let's have a think...
Look at your actions, your intent, and there you might find,
What causes the devil to dance inside of your mind.
Start to consider what bad with good you can adjust,
Because before anyone else it's yourself you must trust.
Take responsibility of what's within your control,
Stop self-medicating and begin to enrol in your soul.
Start now, in this moment before it's too late,
The spiralling demise of your heart shall not be your fate.
Brothers, this is not the time to close up with hate, shame & fear,
Look to both flanks, for you; we are here...

Unknown Infinite Thing

Once I was a soldier,
Now he has gone,
My hollow soul tells me,
An unknown infinite thing

Once I was a soldier,
Don't know who I am,
I know I will never fit in,
The unknown infinite thing.

Once I was a soldier,
Now only the memories of one,
Grief sweeps hot tears onto a cold pillow,
Mourning the unknown infinite thing.

Once I was a solider,
Can I be anyone again,
Stuck in this place forever,
Wishing I had the unknown infinite thing.

❤

Darren Roberts

Moving along gently,
Creeping slow nonstop.
Ticking away quietly
Days turn to night
Night turns to day
This manmade construct,
Slowly burning out...

Neville Johnson

To Be Free Of You

To be free of you,
Yet you have a piece of me,
Always forgotten in the back of your mind,
Except to magnify the faults in your eyes.

Let's take a break,
Even though it does what it says,
What's one more piece of me to miss,
To be free of you.

❤

Darren Roberts

Another Fallen Angel

Shane Glasspool

As the skies alight with fire,
Explosions all around,
The screams of pain strike hard,
On all ears that can be found.
Another man has fallen,
Another life is lost,
Another one to add to the others,
Another fee to pay the cost.
Another fallen friend,
A brother, father, son,
Another hard and weary man,
Whose job for now is done.
Another mother weeping,
Another father comforting all,
Another priest declaring peace,
Another one and all.
Another fallen angel,
To boost Gods mighty force,
When we reach the pearly gates we'll see,
Him standing guard upon white horse. Another fallen angel,
Forgotten by the rest,
The people he defended left him,
To be remembered only by the best.
Another fallen angel,
Another brother we now salute,
Another man who will not live,
To settle your disputes.
Another fallen angel,
God takes only the very best,
To guard the gates to eternal peace,
                                    Where all are free to rest.

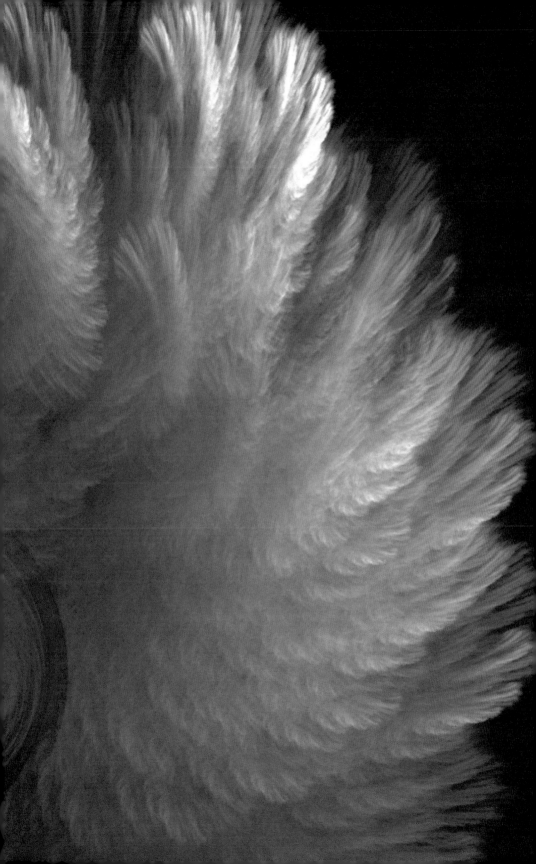

The Soft Silk Of Darkness

Soft silk of darkness so rich,
Depth never ending,
Your emptiness fills everything,
With a smooth caress,

Your honesty so comforting,
No light needed,
The thick void so sweet.
Your silk gliding around me, you're what I need.

Your silent whispers deafen me with memories of
the future,
Days last minutes,
Seconds become hours.

The soft silk of darkness,
Please don't go,
Your the mirror that shows all,
To everyone's soul.

❤

Darren Roberts

Yesterday Will Live Forever

Shane Glasspool

The bullets strafe the ground,
Erupting clouds of dust,
Run fast young soldier,
On your weary legs live or bust.

The sound of rockets fills the air,
Screeching close and then,
Explosions strip the buildings bare,
 And leave the metal bent.

Out of fire and fear you hear it,
So shrill and hurting hard,
The screams of pain from one you love,
He's hit and torn apart.
You see him there,
Not 50m from where you hide,
Clouds erupting all around him,
Save him.... suicide.

He's calling to you,
Come and save me please,
If he could raise himself,
He'd beg you from his knees.

Those around are crawling,
Bodies low as can be made,
Trying to reach their wounded brother,
Who's life must surely be saved.

But to no avail,
Beaten back by fear,
No one can reach him,
No one can get near.

The call for retreat comes over,
And terror grips the heart,
Rush high to your feet and run young soldier,
Your time has come, best start.

Weaving and winding,
You flip and roll,
You sprint fast across the battlefield,
You can hear the funeral toll.

You reach him unscathed,
Drop to your knees and take a grip,
Pull and run and shout for help,
As all around the enemy lets rip.

One last look at his face young soldier,
Study it long and hard,
Blank expression, shock and loss,
This is the truth,
Of how much freedom has cost.

With a scream of hatred,
And sweat pouring fast,
You spring up high in your bed,
How harsh memories last.

3 years now,
Still yesterday stays ,
You did all that you could,
Enjoy what he can't, the rest of your days.

Adrift

Adrift alone,
the touch of warm breeze,
familiar old friend.
Hopelessly lost,
but never so at home.

This ocean of time,
it's endless horizon
A beautiful mirror of souls
Will it take mine?

Adrift in the palms of gods,
familiar old friend,
You know where you're taking me
It's not the end.

♥

Darren Roberts

Have You

Shane Glasspool

Have you felt the mortars falling,
Seen rounds splashing at your feet,
Rockets screeching over your head,
The feeling of defeat.

Have you seen the women running,
Heard the children as they cry,
Looked on and felt so helpless,
As others around you die.

Have you seen the blood come pouring,
From the bodies of your friends,
Have felt the pain of loss,
Wondering when it will ever end.

Have you laid there in the sand,
And listened to the screams,
Watched as life has ebbed away,
Killed all the poor souls dreams.

Have you ran through fire with a stretcher,
To load your dear departed brother,
Sat awake at night,
Wondering what to tell his mother.

Have you returned back home at last,
To the country you keep free,
To be mocked and spat on in the street,
Why did your brothers bleed

.

Have you stood in the graveyard surrounded,
By the memories of the past,
Laying to rest another poor lost soul,
That will by no means be the last.

Have you finished every bottle,
Have you cried long into the night.

Those days a distant memory,
Nothing more than a recollection.
Conversations gone silent,
Two wars in foreign lands.
African bush,
Helmand Valley
Our silence speak a thousand tears,
Walking the same path apart.
Feeling the same pain together.

Neville Johnson

The Darkness & The Light

There's no darkness without the light,
Never knowing each other,
Neither good or bad,
No need to fight.

They can love me and hate
Be silent or loud,
Trap or free me,
Show me my fate.

There's no light without the darkness,
Both are same to me,
Neither bad or good,
Please show me my fate.

❤

Darren Roberts

The wind blowing effortlessly today
It brings more of the same dismay.
Death is here to stay

Neville Johnson

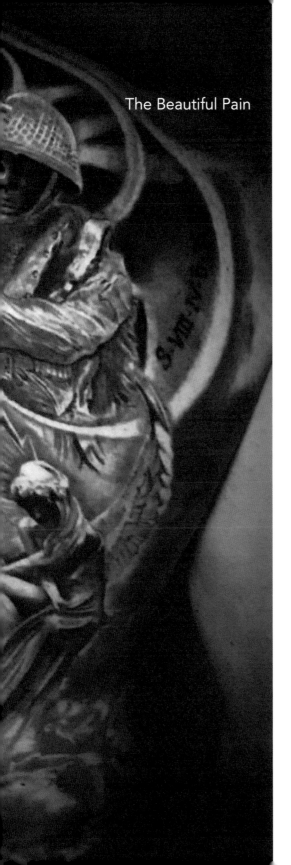

The Beautiful Pain

Beautiful Pain, the needles song
vibrating through my soul.
The black ink on my skin, seeks
truth from the whole.

Alone with the silence, skin
burning with life,
to have something so honest,
my Beautiful Pain.

The orchestra of feelings,
pure and true.
Every stroke of the needle leaving
me whole,
and born again new.

Time slows down and becomes
faster than light.
The hours just seconds and
minutes last a day.
Beautiful Pain why can't you stay.

❤

Darren Roberts

I Stand Alone

Joe Lyne

I stand alone
I stand alone on upon this hill
Myself, morals and my will
My sword gripped in the web of my hand
This is my hill, where I make my final stand
I bow to no man, monster or beast
I pray to no God from the west or the east
I hunted the evil you pretend doesn't exist
I marched in the shadows of the devils abyss
I carried my brothers after their souls departed
I lost my family this is where my hill started
If no man sits at the table where I dine
I can not be poisoned with whispers and wine
This is my hill where I will fight and die
There's no one else here for a tearful goodbye
This is my hill, no place to atone
This is my hill where I stand and die alone

Sangin Valley's dark torrential downpour,
The rain pitter-pattered on the roof.
The sound so utterly mesmerizing.

Neville Johnson

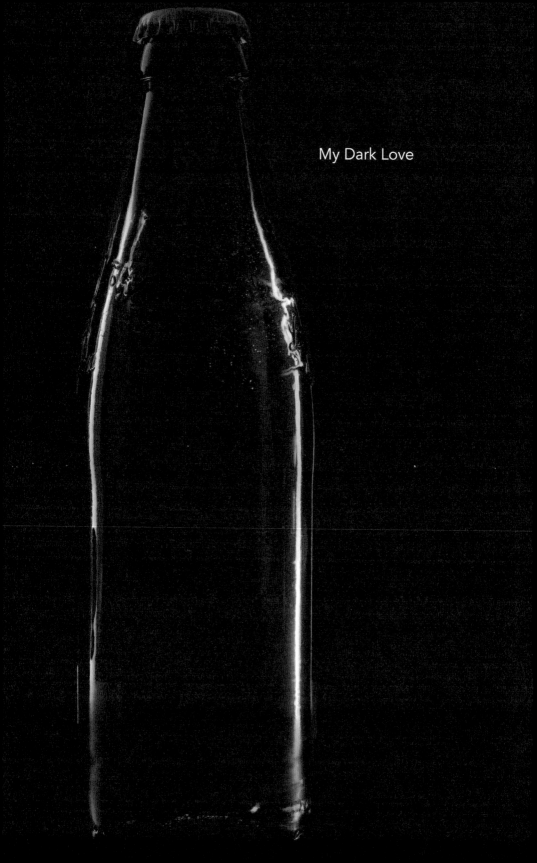

My Dark Love

My Dark Love, her silence rising to a storm,
Mouth dry, heart betraying.
The exhaustion exhilarating, light fading.

The cool reassurance of glass,
The hollow cap echoes.
Firm kiss of burning numbness flows.
The beautiful familiar taste, of stolen fake peace.
My Dark Love.

A pop of false hope, not one but two.
Sharp edges, leaving smooth pearls in my hand.
Harsh plastic in my mouth now,
A flicker of conscious says no.
My Dark Love silken cold burn washes everything away.

I lay down on a cloud, not here or there.
Chest slowing, storm fading.
Too late to turn back now,
My Dark Love of nothing pushing everything away.

I follow her now, as she flows through my veins.
Taking me deeper, away from the pain.
My Dark Love wants to kill me,
I know this is true,
But for just these few hours,
She makes the silence feel true

❤

Darren Roberts

This is not a FIBUA village in the UK, it's an actual town in Bosnia. It was eye opening to see how accurate the FIBUA villages were when I saw the real thing. These are relatively undamaged, a rare sight in Bosnia in those days.

Darren Robers

Why Didn't You Love Me Back

The boy who thinks he's a man,
School tie in the bin,
Signature to run away and finally be home,
I loved you for so long.

Can't shave but have my gun,
Boy soldier, toy soldier,
See how I run,
Bang bang you're dead,
I loved you for so long.

My family of strangers,
Friends with none,
You had my everything,
The boy from home.

You broke and twisted,
Took what you want,
9 years of lifetimes,
I loved you for so long.

❤

Darren Roberts

Good Soldiers Don't Cry

Darren Roberts

What you can't see in this picture is the massive holes in all the roofs, no windows, bullet holes and general destruction of the houses. It did look exactly like a FIBUA Village on Salisbury Plain though, it was so familiar it didn't bother me - which is the point I suppose. Kiss kiss bang bang…

Picture By Darren Roberts

We were in Bosnia, a 6 month tour and as with all things with me in those days I considered it a total waste of my time. If we weren't jumping in and storming villages, why were we there? To be in place as an 'Implementation Force' or 'Stabilisation Force' to allow the country to rebuild itself (after destroying itself) whilst we in the rest of the world watched - I had nothing but contempt for the place. Looking back now of course, this makes no sense to me, it's absolutely terrible and the horrors the population went through are unimaginable.

A couple of months into the tour, a young mum and her toddler turned up at the wire and started talking at me. My Bosnian/Serb/Croat comprised of *'stop, hands up or I shoot'* and *'beer'* so I had to get the interpreter. This was the mid 90's so the use of interpreters was relatively new, we'd been through a big work up (as you always do before a tour) and had gone through some utterly gash scenarios using interpreters at Copehill Down which bore no resemblance to what the reality on the ground ultimately was. It transpired the woman and toddler were there because she feared for their lives, all the men in the village were dead and for whatever reason she found herself on whatever the loosing side was. She said the rest of the village was going to kill her and her kid, she needed sanctuary. My immediate instinct was to tell her to fuck off. If that seems shocking, heartless, cruel or whatever words you want to use - it's because it *absolutely is*.

As a senior Tom it wasn't my call to shelter her or not, I needed a grown up to deal with this, I got one of the seniors up and ultimately she was let in, I was not happy about it. I was firmly of the opinion we should not let her in, because you let one in and then they'll all want to come in. As for her story about the rest of the village wanting to kill them, as far as I was concerned had the situations in the village been reversed she'd be part of the majority wanting to do the same to someone else - so who are we 'protecting' here as they're all as bad as the other. The entire country had destroyed itself on this bullshit, and as a result I'm stood there dealing with this fuckery for 6 months. Writing this now, it is awful. I am awful. It makes no sense.

clashed over it. The two crows on the team had that look on their face when mum and dad start rowing, we really fell out about it - until the next day. Tomorrow was another day and by then she'd been pushed up the line and was someone else's problem. I didn't give her or her kid a second thought.

Why I am telling you this? It's because tragically I feel nothing when I think about it now. I'm married, I have a teenage daughter and consider myself a very empathetic and caring person. Despite this, when I reach back to that moment I still have absolutely no empathy or sympathy for that mum and her toddler. When I reach back to that moment, instead I feel 'nothing', there is simply and empty space where I should feel 'something'. It's like a black hole, 'something' and 'nothing' is there. What should be felt isn't, it's replaced with something else - which is 'no' thing. The sentient cognitive part of me thinks that is abhorrent, it makes no sense to 'me'. Is there a part of my soul missing (or taken), and must still be missing to feel and be this way? Or did I willingly give it? I'm fairly certain that these are psychopathic traits aren't they?

Was it taking me as a 16 year kid, training me to be a soldier, then adult men brutalising me with being forced to drink piss and the constant threat of violence whilst others were beaten in a constant climate of fear as an ongoing rite of passage to be part of the tribe (sprog bashing).? Was it the conflict of me wanting to exist in some sort of Rourkes Drift Lawrence of Arabia poetic conflict when the reality is corrupt geopolitics of foreign policies? How well conditioned (and susceptible?) was I to be able to ignore what should be a moral and ethical crisis?

My best friend didn't react this way so why did I? Is there something wrong with me? Does part of me 'want' to be this way?

I have no way or reasoning or explaining that.

There wasn't a single town or village that wasn't destroyed in Bosnia. Even if it was a remote cottage in the middle of nowhere, it was riddled with bullets and rare to see anything with a roof. To see such destruction of a populated '1st world' country, the systematic genocide that had occurred was like something from the 1940's, not 1990's.

The things people are capable of doing to each other because they are a different religion is beyond my understanding.

Sadly it didn't make me sympathetic or have any compassion towards the population though, just contempt.

Picture By Darren Roberts

The Cruelest Parent

The cruelest parent,
So bitter and tired,
You deserved nothing,
Turned a boy into a broken man.

9 lives I lived,
Before I was free from you,
So much has changed
And everything is the same.

The cruelest parent,
No comfort to give,
Then why do I miss you,
Trying to find a way back.

Beautiful violence,
Friends that I hated,
And wanted to die for,
My closest family,
So desperate for war.

The cruelest parent,
Your darkest heart is my light,
Did you really break me,
Or make me whole again.

Darren Roberts

War Is Not Poetic

Shane Glasspool

In a place where men fight and die,
In a place where fire fills the skies,
Some people think that romance is rife,
That there is poetry in sacrifice.

We see pain misery and rage,
They see a way to fill a page,
Reporters like rats,
Finding brave stories to tell,
Fire questions not rounds,
As they dodge death in our hell.

They tell their stories,
Through their untrained eyes,
They write page after page,
Of ridiculous lies,
Not seeing the truth,
To no soldiers surprise.

There is no poetry in this desolate place,
No unreported bravery,
No hidden disgrace.
No romantic flings,
No love in this war.

Just the spilling of blood,
The death,
And the gore.

Picture By Lee Davies

The Real Cost Of Killing

Shane Glasspool

Taking a life is easy,
Just squeeze the trigger
And follow through.

It's the aftermath thats hard,
The depression,
times of blue.

So many people brag,
And openly exclaim,
They'll kill you if they hate you,
They treat it like a game.

So few of us alive,
Know the true cost that death entails,
We laugh at those who think they know,
If they tried we'd watch them fail.

The cost of taking life,
Isn't easy to explain,
But rest assured you non believers,
It's most certainly not a game.

You commit the action fair and well,
But in due course you grow to find,
The face of your chosen victim,
Rests heavy on your mind.

In times of boredom,
Times of sleep and relaxation,
You'll slide back to that time you squeezed,

Then be hit by devastation.
Uncontrollable emotion,
The inability to sleep,
You'll lay awake for hours and hours,
Not knowing why you weep.

You'll see them across a river,
Hand outstretched and calling loud,
Then wake in a cold sweat,
Screaming out aloud!
You'll drink to kill the dreams,
And only worsen your state of mind,
As your dreams cross borders of reality,
And are constantly on your mind.

You'll see them everywhere,
You'll grow anxious then to rage,
You'll see them in your friends and loved ones,
Even in books they're on the page.

Some are lucky and block this pain,
Others they cannot,
No one has this choice to make,
Once dealt that hand you've got.

The cost of taking life it seems, Is one you can not
measure,
But so you pay the price for killing,
 At your will,
defence and leisure.

Picture By Lee Davies

Soldier Poet Mercenary Saviour

Shane Glasspool

When it called, I answered,
For my country I fell unto my knees.

The time passed quick,
I did what must,
I shed some blood,
I lost some I loved.
That time is gone, that time is past,
A new leaf turned,
The past the past.

My experiences carved in my memory,
I set too to log my thoughts,
The pain that I experienced,
My mind left so distraught.
From the fire of a war a poet there was born,
And one that writes the truth.

These eyes do not lie,
My mind plays no games,
I write my thoughts,
I forget no names.

My dreams are put to paper,
My nightmares not to waste,
I mean to let you all know,
The challenges we face.

Freedom is not free,
Victory is not without pain,
In time you will see,
But a fragment of what has been laid.
I left a soldier,
no skill my country could use,
I turned instead to killing,
Maiming and being used.

For money I now serve,
But neath no flag do my loyalties lie,
For money I am alive,
For money I will die.

A mercenary life for me,
The only one I can pursue,
Its different now I love my life,
I love that I know you.

I made a promise to a chosen few,
That my skills for them I would save,
For if the need arises,
For them my life will be laid.

I break no word, My promise is my oath,
Now matter how distant we become,
Your heart will hold them both.

If you should find in future times,
In danger that you are,
Rest easy in your fear,
And know that I will not be far.

I will be your saviour,
And you my cause to die,
On no other person alive my dear, Are you safer to rely.

From a Soldier in the desert plains,
To a Poet with a heart of pain,
To a Mercenary waiting to be slain,
I would rather die a Saviour,
And live no more with my pain

The further I walk,
The better I feel.
The less I think,
The more I see.
Gaining clarity with each step.

Neville Johnson

Love Is War

Willam FM Currie

My heart is black, my soul is raw.
I never knew Love could be a war.
I Tried to keep her, stay in the battle.
But In the end it doesn't even matter.
Retreating to my trench, I tend to my wounds.
Bury dead emotions, deep in the ground.
Erecting defences, to keep everyone clear.
As commitment is the foe, that I now fear.
When Lovers and Enemies, they all look the same.
How can I bring someone close, risk the pain.
The idea of another bullet, straight through my heart.
To have intertwined souls, torn apart.
So I tread this battlefield carefully,
Taking caution at every turn.
This war hasn't ended, one day I'll find the one.

Alone The Warrior Stands

Shane Glasspool

Alone the weary tiger stood,
Proud before the pearly gates,
For the judgement of St Peter,
He stands and patiently waits.

When along the path of heroes,
St Peter came to cross,
And stared down upon the soldier,
Upon his face a look of loss.

Young man you stand and wait,
But your judgement will not come,
Your entry to this paradise is certain,
For in your life what you have done.

The soldier looked up at him,
Eyes alight with fear,
"But sir, why am I guaranteed a place,
Why am I even here?"
St Peter wept a single tear,
And parted cloudy skies,
Looked down upon the warrior,
And stared deep inside his eyes.

"On earth you fought to defend the weak,
Protected men both beside and behind,
You spoke for the deaf,
And gave eyes to the blind.
You put before your own safety,
The needs of other men,
For this you need never ask permission,
To rest your soul again".

Your war is over soldier,
Stand easy your fight is done,
Come rest now with your brothers.

Your war is over, you have won.

You are here because you stood the test,
You are here because your soul is true,
Now upon these pearly gates,
Your god puts faith in you.

Guard them with your morals,
Protect them with your might,
And when your brothers time comes to join you,
Lead them here with your shining light.

Warriors never die,
They regroup here and lay to rest,
God takes only the bravest of men,
As they guard his gates the best.

Picture: Lee Davies

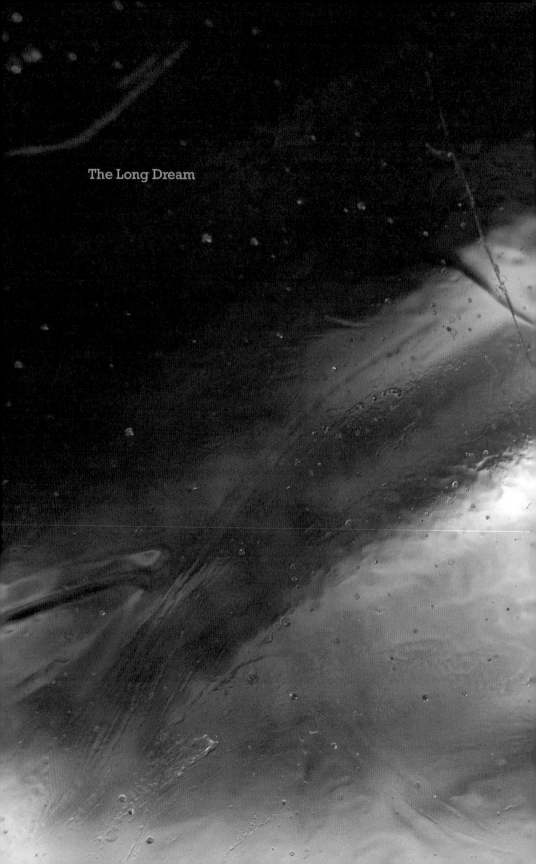

The Long Dream

If sleep is the cousin of Death.
Then every night, A little piece of me dies.
I lay my head down, close my eyes.
Then my consciousness tries process all the lies.
All the deceit, deception and betrayal.
My only hope is I'll wake to tell the tale.

William FM Currie

No One Makes It Out Alive

Noah Miller

Raise that fucking head of yours,
It ain't so hard,
it's just one tour,
Just one tour, now a few more,
Now these tours are a mental war

Facing evil in the eyes,
The horror story of my life,
I lost my innocence, and my wife,
Sitting, staring, glaring, at my knife...

Arriving home, full of lies,
"Oh, you're so kind,
But no I'm fine..."
My clock is ticking,
I'm out of time.

This mountain has no other side,
It'll always be an uphill climb,
Oh, Don't be fooled,
You might have survived,
but will you actually ever be alive?

•NEVER FORGET•

Rob Creighton

In a time before our father's birth
A boy left home to prove his worth,
His mission to use good to fight evil
To protect our lands, seas, air & people,
Then stood in boots with putties wrapped,
Weapon in hand and his equipment strapped,
He acts on orders from left and right,
To go over the top and start his fight,
With fear and courage mixed in one cry,
He runs forward with his demise flying by,
Men succumb to slaughter all around,
To lay dead & dying on sacred ground,
The offensive fails and the battle lulls,
And this dark day now somehow further dulls,
Whilst in the aftermath of stench & death,
He spots his brother gasping for breath,
Kneeling at his side as the low sun starts to set,
And through blooded lips he whispers;

"Never Forget".

As I close my eyes I drift to that place,
The smell, the sound so reverberating.
The distinctive roaring vibration.
Sound of hope...

Dust covered faces, hands caked in blood.
The smiles on their faces.
Death behind those eyes, oh those eyes,
Those eyes, cold death filled eyes.
Crying and laughing with these over powering
emotions.
Their empty vessels overflowing,
Filling them to the brim.

Neville Johnson

I've got Murder on my mind.
Horrific images from deep inside.
Going round and round like a carousel ride.
Dark intrusive thoughts poison my time.

I envisage the act, what would it take?
Contemplating the ways a human body breaks.
How a person responds to bouts of extreme pain.
Or the way that blood flows like the words from my pen.

Screams of torture, my victim howling in despair.
Clawing, at a rope tied neck, gasping for air.
Sharp bladed tools, dragged across raw skin.
Tearing holes in the body to release the sin.

I'm the murderer, the killer, deaths architect.
Held in my grasp they'll be no escape.
The soul of my victim is the last thing I'll take.
The slaughter, the bloodshed, I'll never regret.

Who'll be the victim, whose death I'll orchestrate.
This execution is mine, I've chosen my fate.
The clock has stuck,so now its my time.
I've got murder on my mind and that murder is mine.

Murderous Mind

Willam FM Currie

Carolyn Jones

She Soldier

Standing on that parade square,
Bile runs down my cheek,
I stand in shame,
My face red hot,
I feel drool drop from my chin,
Onto my freshly pressed army greens,
As a Sergeant Major shouts
'At ease...'
I sway from foot to foot,
Trying to relieve the weight,
The pressure of standing,
For over 3 hours,
Enduring endless insults,
I do not want to go home,
be a hairdresser,
be a baby sitter,
Find a husband,
I am here, I am strong, I am proud

999 SERVICES

Rob Creighton

To the thief takers and heart breakers,
The smoke eaters and death cheaters,
The peace keepers and grim reapers,
The door kickers and crook trickers,
The door breachers and lesson teachers,
My brothers from other mothers,
And my sisters from other misters,
We are one.

Every Lie has Consequences

You created these animals with a vicious bite.
Then send them to war to fight your fight.
Once they've done the deed, secured your win.
Now you turn your back on them, say they've sinned.

But you've never had to walk a day in their shoes.
Never had to carry their weight or bear the bruises.
There's this mark that war leaves ingrained.
Deep within their unconscious brain.
A stain, a taint, a nagging pain.
As they reminisce of the enemy, that they've slain.

Now you sleep peacefully, your conscience is clear.
Yet veterans are tormented waking with brutal nightmares.
Your decision to lie, take this country to war.
Is why warriors commit suicide to end it all.

Willam FM Currie

Picture By Lee Davies

Words

Unspoken words that we never said.
These unspoken words, locked within my head.
Regret over words, I'd liked to have shared.
Words to show you, how much I cared.
Those words may have created, a stronger tie.
We could have been bonded by words till the day we died.
Maybe you had words, but I can only speculate.
Your unspoken words, but I guess it's too late
Our words unspoken began at the start
Unspoken words, so our hearts drifted apart.
No words now, so the silence is deafening.
As I reflect on these words, I guess this is my lesson.

William FM Currie

Picture By Lee Davies

Pick Your Poison

Ben Fleming

I once missed the days of disarray,
Convinced I was at home in the fray,
I never knew life until death was chasing me,
I was so addicted to the game,
He became afraid to play with me,
My lust for chaos was deafening,
I confess my vice was adrenaline.

The Devil

Steven Shepherd

Show me someone 100% pure and innocent
And I'll show you the Devil
The devil that lurks within all I have met
His control varies but its ever there
Some just hide him better
I can hide him well
But not from myself
Pour me a Whisky
Cut me a line
I'll pull you in
And i'll tell you all about it...

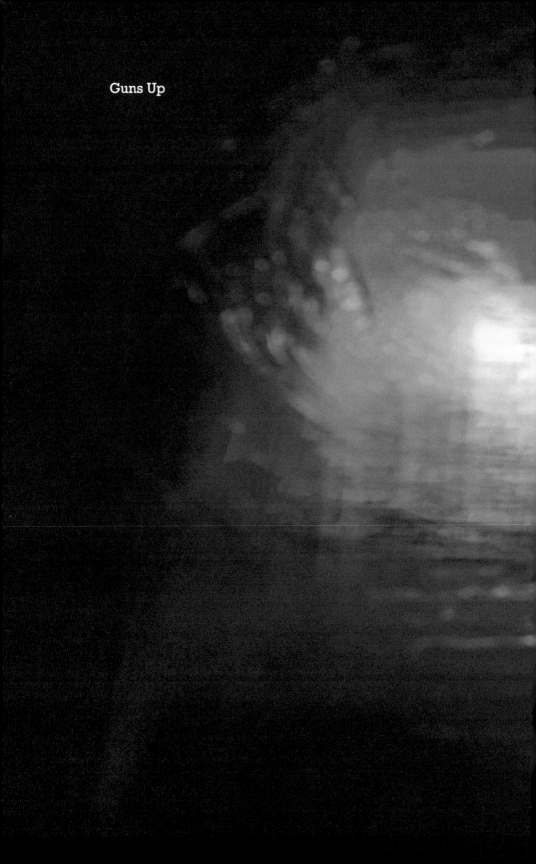

Guns Up

Willam FM Currie

I'm a bad mother fucker.
So when the bells toll for
thee.
Whether your hiding on
land or at sea.
When I knock at your
door, It won't be gently.
But with the full wrath of
god, I'm here to serve
your penalty.
Like the 4 horseman of
the apocalypse or a
shadowy grim reaper.
I'll ensure you'll meet
your keeper.
That terrifying image of
me, you'll never forget.
As you answer for your
sins, Pay your debt.
It'll haunt your soul, until
the end of time.
For I was the executioner,
when you paid for your
crimes.

This was how most towns & villages looked in
Bosnia, roofless and shot to pieces.

Darren Roberts

I Have Questions

Willam FM Currie

As I sit here patiently waiting,
Contemplating.
Trying to figure out the answers, to the questions I've never asked.
Speculating if the meaning of life, will ever be within my grasp.
The questions are but scrambled thoughts, deep within my mind.
One day they may make sense to me, but now is not the time.
Their words have yet to breach my lips, so their stories are yet untold.
One day these questions may make sense to me, but for now I just
grow old.

What are all these questions? I think that you may ask.
In time I'll explain my ramblings, regarding my futile task.
I hope,
in time,
some of my madness will be unmasked.
So finally, you will understand, what I'm on about at last.

But for now I have a question for you, if I just could be so bold?
I will try to convey a message, as you listen to it unfold.
Please don't be upset, by my point of view, that I'm going to deliver.
You may feel the need to debate me on this, I shalt never quiver.

So to start this discussion, a little faster,
I'm posing this question as the starter.

How to you intend to present yourself when reaper calls your name?
Will you cower in a corner, panicked with your guilt and shame?
When you realise that your life dictates, your entrance to Heaven.
That our morals are more important than Money, Fame or Possessions.

Explain yourself, you'll need to do.
whilst standing at gates.
On how you have conducted your life.
And possessed all of these traits?

Life.
  Protector.
    Destroyer.
     Evil.
      Good.
       Angel.
        Sinner.
         Loser.
          Winner.
Death.

How can one embrace, that they're moral within?
When their life is riddled, with so much unseen sin!
You think good deeds, should get you an applause?
With all the pain, agony and destruction that you've caused.
Hidden deep inside your soul are the atrocities that gnaw.

What if it told you?

That good deeds don't eliminate the bad, no law of average applies.
as we wonder through this life, telling all ourselves these lies.
Worried if your found out, you'll be tainted and despised.
No longer looked upon, by those affectionate eyes.

All people have these qualities, which inflict upon them emotional
pain.
So, don't beat yourself up, don't cause yourself, any shame.
We're all but creatures upon this earth, caught in this waiting game.
Dreading the day were put to rest, then the devil tries to claim.

Each of us so different, but we share the biggest Sin.
I wonder if this excuse will work, and St Peter lets us in.
The sin is that, we're only Human!
I'll say it with a grin!

Confiscated weapons - Bosnia mid 90's

Darren Roberts

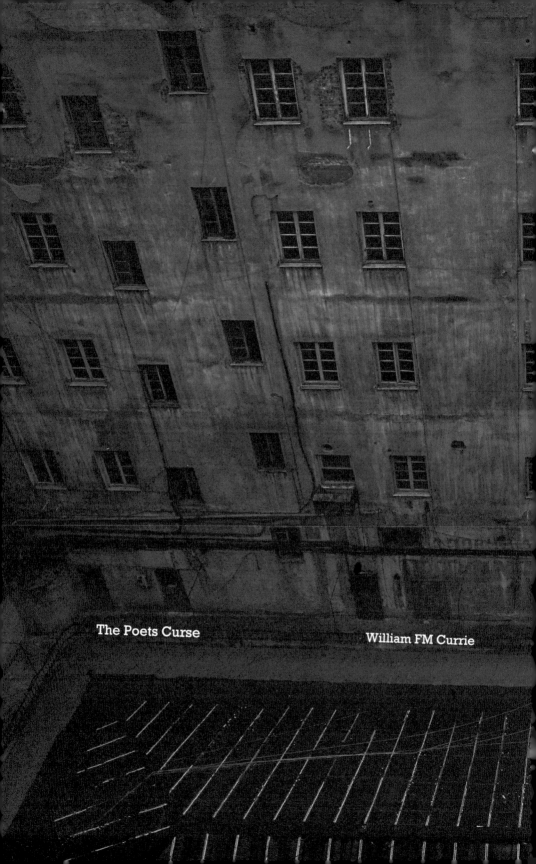

The Poets Curse

William FM Currie

I visit hades where my demons congregate.
Even in the air, I can smell the evils hate.
They argue over who gets to devour my soul.
Who will be the one that keeps me In this Hole.
I have to tread quietly, incorporate my guile.
To save my sanity, I'm here a short while.
In the darkness of hades is
where my creativeness grows.
So I grab some inspiration,
then I need to go.
Caught down here,
is at my mental
health's demise.
Is dancing
with my
demons,
really
worth
this
poetic
prize.

A Lost Love

Ben Fleming

Mind wrestles between right and wrong,
Of what remains and what is gone,
War and peace and all that follows,
A mind so full a heart so hollow,
To feel is blunted I acquiesce,
Pondering why is it, the war I miss?

Picture By Lee Davies

When the sands run low

The soldiers road

The never ending chase
a forever changing pace

Hand in hand go the wise finds
Always pursued by weary minds

Battered bodies can not amplify
Unless there's a breath and a sparkle in the eye

When the wolf stands snarling at the gate
Flare the nostrils and attack with hate

And when you return flying your bloodied banner
When life has changed beyond all known manner

When you no longer fit among this world of men
Because you are a man of the sword and not of the pen

Do not yield or capitulate
Do not be consumed by the hate

For you have walked in the devils stride
But you are not yet welcome where angels reside

For now you return where hostilities cease
This is the time to find your peace

The lessons you learned along the way
It's too good to leave and too bad to stay

To endure the pain and ask for more
To need no wealth and be content with poor

Live your days without regret
Because the hangman's toll is not yet set

When death calls stand proud and steady
Stare the bastard in the eye and say I'm ready

Joe Lyne

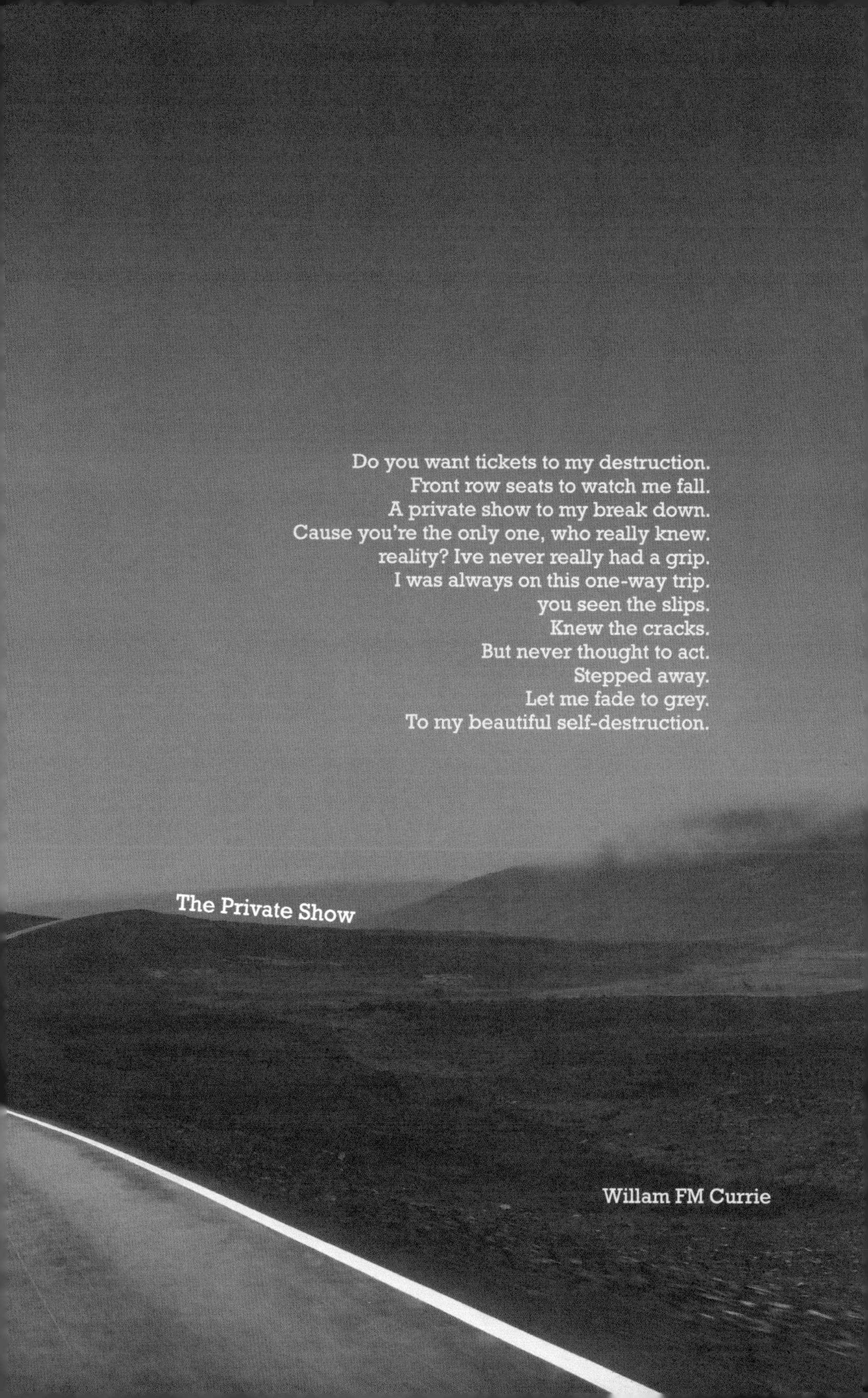

Do you want tickets to my destruction.
Front row seats to watch me fall.
A private show to my break down.
Cause you're the only one, who really knew.
reality? Ive never really had a grip.
I was always on this one-way trip.
you seen the slips.
Knew the cracks.
But never thought to act.
Stepped away.
Let me fade to grey.
To my beautiful self-destruction.

The Private Show

Willam FM Currie

Ben Fleming

The Untouchables Touched

Here I am beneath these stars,
Reminded again how I got these scars,
Only visible in the dark,
Can't deny that war leaves a mark.

• C R A S H •

Rob Creighton

Vehicles collide, pain supplied;
~Savagely.

Limbs peeled, anatomy revealed;
~Mechanically.

Lives battered, futures tattered;
~Tragically.

Rescue tendered, saviour rendered;
~Rapidly.

Hope evaporated, time terminated;
~Desperately.

I looked it in the eyes,
That was the start of my demise.
Those dreadful cries,
Raining down,
He was a master of disguise.

Neville Johnson

Picture By Lee Davies

Battlefield Taxi

Ben Fleming

We meet on the melting tarmac,
Scorching heat hazes the view,
A rolling carcass of steel and Kevlar,
Mother of the fleet, she carries us all,
Washes our face in warmth as we board,

Loud whine as she strains with the load,
Grows louder still as she rises above,
Look out the bulbous windows at the earth below,
Heaved to a halt on her back toes a firm thud,
Ramp lowers letting the outside in and the inside out.

Picture By Joe Lyne

Man soldier monster

When the wolf is at the gate
There is no longer time to contemplate

Men of duty hear the call
The glory of Valhalla's hall

They take up arms next to each other
That solid embrace that is a brother

The noble cause to fight for the free
As the fog draws down the cause is hard to see

At first they kill only to save another
The noble soldier who was born of a mother

Emotion fades just like every sun
When instinct takes over the change has begun

Thought and reason dissipate away
The blood lust races you into the fray

There are no longer thoughts of family or friend
There is only a pure hatred a man can not
comprehend

This is the truth and the free are unaware
But this is conflict when all is stripped bare

There is no place in battle for any reprieve
There is no time to stop and grieve

It's only a time to summon the gross and vile
To line up the beasts as one rank and file

For when comes a time to destroy and conquer
It is only a time for man to become monster

Joe Lyne

I Stood Where You Died

Ben Fleming

I stood where you died,
It was quiet and free of war when I stood where you died.

The earth was undisturbed and free, there was no blood like I expected to see,
But a smog loomed, a grey feeling, it stuck to our minds as the patrol was kneeling.

A rag tied to bushes fluttered innocently in the wind,
But how many rags taunt twenty-year-old men.
In words of its own whispers to us, "here a young soul was dimmed",
When I stood where you died, there was an odourless stench.

In the trench to the left, the remnants of a horn laid,
No search could prevent death prevailing that day,
And so it served as a reminder on every patrol,
The truth, that none of us are in control.

Never did I really think back to that scene I described,
Until I saw your Dad and the pain in his eyes,
How he missed playing games of chess,
And how he wanted to see the spot where you died.

It shook me much more than that place,
To see the look on a fathers face,
Parts of me wanted to show him that route,
To tell him we killed as many enemy as we could shoot.

It's not my place I realised,
There is little solace I could provide,
With the fact, that I had stood where you died.

Rob Creighton

•IGBALA•

Now this is one that will stay with me,
Clear, crisp and raw was the night.
The darkness was deep and forever,
Only broken by flames and blue light.

Arriving at scene I saw you;
There in the grass where you lay at rest.
Your small lifeless body,
Cold to the touch,
No beating inside of your chest.

Your soft brown skin was unbroken,
Were you simply asleep all along?
With my hand I keep pumping your heart in hope,
that the facts all around me are wrong.

I've seen your face a thousand times since;
So often it feels you're a friend,
Each time I wonder what would have been of your
life; If what was broken that night I could mend...

The tear rolls down my hardened face
My absent brothers I can't embrace

We left together to fight the war
We don't talk of the things we saw

For average folk they won't understand
Why the blood was shed into the sand

Not for politics, freedom or fate
Not against tyranny and not for hate

We fought for each other like good brothers do
That's as simple as war gets for me and you

And pausing today when the clock strikes eleven
I think of my brothers in Valhalla and heaven.

Only fighting in war can forge such a bond
Through the mud and blood to the green fields beyond

FEAR NAUGHT

Absent Brothers

Joe Lyne

• C R A S H • (pt 2)   Rob Creighton

Sweet metallic smell of reaping lingers in frigid air,

Grey furnishings crimsoned by thick creeping flow,

My dappled light catches sight of callous tears,

Souls now dim where once they used to glow.

Ben Fleming

This Is Where I Fell

Shane Glasspool

This is where I fought my final fight,
This is where my life did end,
This is where I walked into the light.

This solid lonely rifle,
Mounted sturdy in the ground,
Marks the spot where I was taken,
Where my end was finally found.

As you pass me by and stare,
Spare a thought for me in your prayers,
For I will not see my home again,
Like many others will not see theirs.

Do not cry for me though brothers,
Please do not shed a tear,
I went down into the underworld,
Whilst holding back my fear.

As you pass this place don't halt,
Don't wonder who I was,
Just know that for the freedom of many,
My life was finally lost.

I did not hesitate to stop,
Whilst running up this hill,
Did not sympathise the enemy,
The men I had to kill,
I only thought of home,
And those that I once loved,
Now I think of them in the heavens,
From the starry skies above.

I look down upon you with admiration,
As the tears well up in my eyes,
I wish I had been left to live,
To fight there by your sides.
But alas my skills were needed,
By a commander greater than our own,
And on this lofty perch I'll watch you,
And make sure you are guided safely home.

Picture: Lee Davies

I remember that it hurt him more,
He needed me more than before.
I failed him in a time of need.
I failed him as a father,
You deserve better,
not the stranger you see.
My son,
Be better than me.
Be more than me.

Neville Johnson

Staying In The fight

The invisible and unknown enemy,
Cannot be seen or heard,
Just a feeling or thought,
Fight through the ambush when it comes,
Take the initiative and win the fight.

The invisible unknown enemy,
Seen in the mirror every day,
The endless battlefield of my mind,
Me against me,
A victory for who.

Am I the enemy or the saviour,
Am I winning or loosing,
The battle, the fight, the war,
With myself or everyone else.

Stay in the fight.

It's all I know.

❤

Darren Roberts

This is a wonderful life,
Said the father to his son.
But the memories,
They don't match his smile.
He's eyes are heavy,
With these memories.
This is a wonderful life,
My son, this life you live.
Said the father to his son.
Heaviness to his coat today,
It was absent the year before.
This is a wonderful life,
Said the father to his son.
A wonderful wild...

Neville Johnson

Ben Fleming

I reminisce,
Because I miss.
Daydreaming and thinking,
The Sangin sound so
reverberating..

Neville Johnson

Untying The Knot

Pressure builds,
Compressing in my chest.
The knot tightens,
Everyone has their hand.

The iron knot,
in my heart,
my soul.

Where do I start?
How will you go?

Darren Roberts

•COURAGE•

Rob Creighton

It's often said that "courage is not in the absence of fear but in spite of it"....for courage to come into action there must be the overwhelming presence of fear.

Courage is action & decision placed boldly in the face of pain, danger, uncertainty or intimidation.
Courage is a positive reaction against a negative force.
Simply put; it is Good versus Evil.

Often courage isn't like it is portrayed in literature or film.
Real courage can be applied under hesitation and trembling limbs.
The heart is strong, the head is willing but the physical 'doing' does not come naturally to the individual,
who's shoulders on which the responsibility of action is bestowed.

If courage is ever required of you: Good Speed.

Ben Fleming

Be Free My Brother

Be free my brother,
The prison of our minds doesn't have to be,
Smash the walls bricked with the expectations of others,
The storm is calling us,
Loving thunder crushing the lies of the world ,
Lightning tearing the sky with the light of our truth.
What others fear all you see is love,
Beautiful violence of nature's chaos,
Be free my brother, don't you see?
You don't need or have to be,
The soldier out of time anymore,
It's time to rise and be free,
Let the storm take you,
It will bring you to me,

Be free my brother.

Be free with me.

Darren Roberts

After the fear,
After the painful goodbyes.
The pain of coming home

Neville Johnson.

Picture By Lee Davies

Soul Of My Soul

Where do I stop and you begin,
Infinite filaments intertwined so,
Am I you and you me,
Can either of us hold the other in.

Soul of my soul,
The mirror of our universe,
Do we want to see,
Something we already know.

Hold me now don't let go,
Soul of my soul,
Now we know,
Infinite emotions intertwined so.

❤

Darren Roberts

• BUILD DISCIPLINE •

Rob Creighton

Discipline is not a random fleeting moment or drippy emotion,
nor is it a thing you can simply pick up where ever you abandoned it.
You can't use it like a crutch whenever you feel the urge to do things you have not readied for.

Discipline is not a materialistic accessory to adorn yourself in because it sounds good,
looks good or ticks a box.
It can not be faked, falsified or feigned.
Never pretend to be disciplined,
you will be found out almost immediately.

Discipline is not free or simple; it is not easy and it is not for the feint hearted.
Those who are meagre in their application and sloppy in their execution can not tame it.
It takes time, repetition and habit.
But it can harnessed.

Discipline needs to be built; it needs to be built brick by brick,
course by course until it's a big fucking impenetrable fortress.
Your fortress.

Now, Don't be scared by discipline; Take hold of it and place it beside you.
Arm yourself to the back teeth with it and move courageously forward with it.

Never stop moving forward with it.

Discipline will change you.

My Strawberry Lemonade

Pillow smells of strawberry,
Lemonade and peach,
My everything to me,
Together we will be,
Forever and always,
Please tell me it's meant to be,
You're as fucked up as me.

♥

Darren Roberts

Picture By Lee Davies

Share & Grow

Share and grow,
My servants heart,
Sleeve worn out,
It's taken me apart.

Share and grow,
So much to give,
Has too much been taken,
Only my god can know.

Share and grow,
A love that can't be spoken,
To rest the weary servant,
Surely you must know.

Darren Roberts

Do you remember, last September?
Before the fall, before it all?
The destruction, the lost connection,
The lost for all.
Do you still remember, their faces?
The smiles and memories.
Dust smeared faces, wrinkles and all.
Memories fade, yet do we remember,
Before the...
The loss of all of us
Do we remember?

Neville Johnson

Natures sound subdued to a whisper,
A heaviness to my soul today
It was absent the day before.
Her exquisite glow illuminate my grey
existence.

Her golden vibrant rays,
Gives bright color the clouds and mountains.
Filing the sky with shades of pink, peach
and amber.

Color so ever gentle for the soul,
She brings hope of a new beginning.
Just like yesterday and the day before.
She will bring the same tomorrow,
Hope for all.

Neville Johnson

The Life You Have

Grieving the life lost,
That I hated,
Bothers no more,
But never were,
There's so much more,
My eyes are open,
A life just begun,
Filled with choices.

❤

Darren Roberts

Give Me

Steven Shepherd

Give me a Foreign land
Give me a unfamiliar culture
Give me uncertainty
Give me a loaded weapon
Give me the possibility
Give me that adrenaline high
Give me that buzz
Give me that fight
Give me bitter sweet memories
Give me war

The Lost Boy In Me

The lies we believed so readily and easily,
My perfect neverland for lost boys like me,
Never grow up, never ever cry,
The lost boy needs those beautiful lies.

❤

Darren Roberts

I Once...

Joe Lyne

I once travelled to the most beautiful land I've ever seen
Hunting the worst evil I've ever known
With the bravest men I've ever met.
I once became the monster you only read in stories
Fighting with a violence I never thought possible
With a hatred so pure I couldn't describe with words
I once loved brothers closer than the blood spilled between us
Finding something to laugh about every single day
I was part of a large loyal family of misfits to the crown
I once was ... but now I am not

20 Again

Steven Shepherd

To be 20 again
Boy not a man
Patrolling a war torn land
Contact wait out
Eyes up
Find the firing point, here on the map
3 rounds fire for effect
Shot boss, it's on its way
I'm 20, should someone check my work?
No don't worry
You're no longer a boy
Smash it
Self defence, Card Alpha
Regardless of age

A life already lived,
Things seen and done,
So much to forget,
Yet this is not the end.

So much lost,
Taken and not given,
Unwanted and forgotten,
But it's not the end.

Silk threads of hope,
Can connect me to the stars,
So much more to dream,
We can start anew.
This is not the end.

Brothers to meet,
Lost in neglect,
Let's shed our burdens,
Write a new story,
This is not the end.

Curiousness of infinite night,
Laugh at the moon,
Embrace the loving dawn,
My beautiful brothers,
This is not the end.
❤

Darren Roberts

This Is Not The End

•THE RICHER MAN•

Rob Creighton

The recompense for your service is meagre,
The coin is light and the hours can be forever.
But I would question the moral fibre of any man
who would prefer such shallow reward in place of a
life full of honour & pride within a service steeped
in valour & history,
All whilst amongst those whom would risk all for
you and you for them...
I ask you again; who is the richer man?

• T R I B E •

"Build your tribe, love them hard"

Rob Creighton

• L O V E D •

"With the stars out of his reach and the oceans too
vast for him to tackle she ignited a fire in his heart
that made anything possible…"

Rob Creighton

Picture By Lee Davies

As Much as Things Change. They Stay the Same.

Ben Fleming

Robert and William fired through loopholes in the walls as hundreds of enemy closed in on the hospital. The rate of fire had been so unrelenting that the barrels began to scorch their hands. Ammunition was waning and the enemy drew closer. As one continued to fire, the other began breaking through the wall with his bare hands in order to drag the patients through to the next room. By this point the enemy had enclosed their position and began making entry to the hospital. Robert Jones defended the doorway with his bayonet, engaging in a ferocious and desperate hand to hand battle in order to protect the extraction of the patients. The doorway was nearly full of dead or wounded enemy by the time he was finished.

The hospital was now engulfed with smoke. The heat of the fire overwhelming. He and William Jones having retrieved six of the casualties, Robert went back for the seventh and final casualty, Sergeant Maxfield, refusing to leave anyone behind. Despite the smoke and heat that tried to beat him back, it didn't obscure his view as the blades were plunged into Sergeant Maxfield's body. He witnessed the Zulu frenzy as clear as day. He witnessed Maxfield's mutilation in plain sight. He watched the life drain from his body on the bed as he looked on helplessly. This was the British Army's 2nd Battalion, 24th of Foot, defence at Rorkes Drift, or thanks to the 1964 film, what most will simply know as "Zulu".

Private Robert Jones VC was twenty one years old. He was a hero. He saved lives. He was held up by his colleagues. Awarded the highest gallantry medal the British Army has, the Victoria Cross. Yet nineteen years after this action the muzzle end of a shotgun seemed to make so much sense to him that he took his own life. He had survived an aggressive fire, smoke inhalation, being stabbed four times, shot once, but eventually he succumbed to the deepest wound of the war. His own mind.

His wife told the coroner how his experiences of war came to haunt him at night in the form of nightmares. I'm sure he still smiled at his five children. I'm sure he still loved his wife. I'm sure he laughed with his friends over a beer. I'm sure he sported his four assegai scars with an element of pride. But I'm also sure he never said anything of the mental scars of war. For fear of judgement. Yet judgement still came, just after his death.

Robert Jones's courage, fortitude, distinguished career and gallantry awards were quickly forgotten. The coroner judged him temporarily insane on the day he borrowed his employers shotgun. He was viewed as taking "the cowards way out". A British War Hero. Robert was treated with such disdain for losing his battle to the invisible wounds of war that his coffin was forced to enter the churchyard over the wall. Perhaps worst of all is Roberts headstone, deliberately placed facing away from the Church and other headstones, a lasting reminder of the attitude displayed to his struggles and his death. I doubt he was the first to lose his battle and he certainly isn't the last.

In the time since the Anglo-Zulu War we've got better at mental health. I think. Until I start really thinking about what's changed and what hasn't. We talk, but usually only once we've reached the point of spinning out. We say that people can come forward for help without judgement, before suspending them from their duties. We tell our friends that they can talk to us anytime "just call me", but when they do, we often cower away from the conversation when faced with the uncomfortable truth. "My friend is in a bad way". Is it intentional? I think not. Instead I am reminded how most react at news of a casualty or loss of a loved one. Denial. "No it can't be". "But we cleared that area how could he get hit?" "We're home now, how could the war still be effecting them?" We as individuals are trying to cope. If we acknowledge the issue it becomes real. That's what we shy away from facing.

On the flipside we've got better at push ups. Our hashtags of support get evermore creative and our leaders do the "medicine ball challenge", carrying it around to spread "awareness". At this point if you were unaware that Veterans and service members are still killing themselves, every single day, let me know which rock you live under.

I poke fun at these sentiments and challenges but that's all I do. I recognise that by and large they are the well intended actions of good people. The reality however is we've got good at saying the right things but fail to live by them. How many of us are guilty of taking part in these challenges but fail to say when something is wrong? In almost all the cases I know, we wait until breaking point. At that point though it's 50/50, a first step in the pursuit of betterment or a final step like Robert Jones.

We see that friend who we haven't spoken to in far too long post something on their social media. We know their post isn't normal. We're the masters of noticing the abnormal. We can spot a pressure plate in the ground from the discoloured earth that sits above it. But instead of reacting to it like we would on operations, we "like" it and hope that's all that's needed. We turn a blind eye and hope that IED doesn't go off. Perhaps it's the modern day equivalent of facing the headstone the other way. We shy away from what is probably the only noble fight we'll ever know. What could be our brother or sisters breaking point, we leave them to figure out which fork in the road to take. Alone.

We are all a little like Robert Jones VC even if we think we're not. We carry the wounds of war long after we've come home. We think we've locked it all away deep in the locker. We smile at our children. Love our partners. Enjoy a beer with our friends. Waiting until we reach the fork in the road. Hoping that when we get there we make the right choice, but we won't talk about it. Instead we'll bullshit ourselves that there's some form of nobility for suffering in silence and we'll bullshit our friends we're good. Until we can call ourselves out on that bullshit, the reality will always be that as much as things change. They stay the same.

Picture By Lee Davies

Driving from Croatia up into Bosnia - mid 90's

Darren Roberts

Belize 1994 - Nothing fucks the allyness of a picture up more than a BFA. However I failed to get many pictures of the live firing whilst in the jungle. I also didn't cut my hat down, I decided to not have things falling down the back of my neck instead.

Darren Roberts

Thanks for taking the time to read this book, I hope that it's helped in some way with a sense of shared feeling. No one is coming to help us, we have to help ourselves - but that doesn't mean you have to do it on your own. As with the first book, this has been an incredible journey. It's comforting to read others words and find reflection in them - it means we are not alone. Again I can't thank everyone enough for contributing their work, the authenticity and emotion is there for all to see.

What probably comes across is despite everything no matter how bad things were, there's a part of us that would go back if we could.

I still have no way of reasoning or explaining that.

No one wants a massive pity party, that doesn't help anyone. I also have made my feelings very clear that one of the worst groups of people when it comes to how veterans are treated, are other veterans - without a doubt we can be our own worst enemies. However having a voice, an outlet and a platform to make feelings known can help.

A loss I didn't expect to experience, and spent 15 years either ignoring or not realising - was my military service. Having set the land speed record out of the camp gates after being discharged from 9 years service in 1998 - I was overjoyed. Except I wasn't going 'towards' anything, I was 'getting away' from something and that's a massive difference There were a lot of things to enjoy in my time and be proud of. We got to do some really cool things - but ultimately I succumbed to the complete fuckery of dysfunctional military leadership and left. Being so utterly focused on *not being in* anymore meant I didn't mourn the loss of the life I'd had from boy to man, which would enable me to move on in the life I now have.

It's ok to miss it, that doesn't mean I missed it all - however the thing or things I did miss needed to be 'mourned' because it's part of me that's gone. There's a loss that needs to be come to terms with - once I'd started to do that, I've been able to move on. Camaraderie, banter and brotherhood. All these things we had are taken away when we leave. I was so focussed on getting away I cut off most contact with most people, that's not difficult when you're 100's miles away and they're on Tour most years. Then it's 20 years later, the hole which I papered over is left wide open and I've no how idea to fill it. This might not make any sense to anyone - all I can say is 15 years after leaving is when it got to me, and I think it touches everyone eventually whether it's 5, 10, 15 or 20 years later.

A big learning over last couple of years is you don't have to loose that brotherhood you once had, if you're open to it. New connections can be made, a new circle, a new tribe. Maybe they're veterans and maybe they're not - they are out there though, just like you. They feel isolated, alone and closed off to the civilian world of bullshit around them. They're kindred spirits, connecting with them isn't some lame as fuck exercise in rose tinted glasses wearing blazer and Regt tie drinking piss warm flat beer in the legion. It's not a disingenuous bullshit-fest of 'how good it all was' because large portions of it were staggeringly awful. They share the same interests, jokes and outlook on life. I've made a few new friends, and they're friends for life - a new brotherhood. Who you'd go to war with and who'd go with you, even if they're a civvie.

You just need to be open…

Darren

• ANNA •

• A N N A •

Hero WoD: Dedicated to ARV Officer Anna SMITH (38) of Thames Valley Police.

"ANNA"

(Partnered Wod w/ 10kg vest)

-1mile run (or 100 double unders)
-90 x Box Jump Overs (24/20)
-80 x Kb Swings (24/16)
-70 x Burpees
-60 x Wall Balls
-50 x Plate OH Lunges (15/10)
-40 x Toes 2 Bar
-30 x Kb Snatches (24/16)
-20 x Pull Ups
-1mile run (or 100 double unders)
-Repeat back up ladder.

Anna was a Police Officer, a Wife & a Mother. She tragically lost her year long battle with cancer on 7th June 2018, she was just 38.

Her husband Ed is rowing the Atlantic next year in her memory of his wife and to raise money for @victoriaspromise who supported Anna throughout her hard fought battle.

Head over to @doitforanna for further details.

"Every day may not be good but there is something good in every day"

~Alice Morse Earle.

NUNQUAM NON PARATUS